This book belongs to

_____,

who is awesome and amazing.

YOU ARE AMONG FRIENDS

Advice for the Little Sisters I Never Had

Lindsey Markel

ISBN 978-0-557-21817-2

"Any woman who chooses to behave like a full human being should be warned that the armies of the status quo will treat her as something of a dirty joke. That's their natural and first weapon. She will need her sisterhood."

—Gloria Steinem

Don't be afraid,
don't be afraid,
don't be afraid,
don't be afraid!

CONTENTS.

We are the only ones who decide who we are. Our ideas of ourselves and our abilities are what define our world and guide us in making our choices. And it's reassuring to have a set idea of who you are. It is not always easy to demand the best for yourself—to ask for what you really want while believing that you deserve it. It is easy to think of yourself as a person who is average, not that great at much but not bad either, because being average is a great way to get by.

I am not interested in speaking to you in a way that encourages you to be average.

You are not average.

You must believe *only* the truth about yourself; you have to choose to believe it now, and fight against the forces that want you to believe the lie of anything otherwise.

You are extraordinary.

But what you don't know is that you are extraordinary already. You don't have to be scared of working hard at being great and then failing. You have bravery and beauty and all the softness and boldness in the world already in you, built into the dust you were sculpted from.

Things are going to change for you. This will be true for you at most stages of your life, as far as I can tell at this point in mine, but when you are young, and when things first begin to change, it's easy to feel lost. You are changing quickly—your body, your hormones, your perception of the world and your perception of yourself—but even as you change, you yearn for the comfort of familiar things, and the ones most familiar might seem distant at times.

You will feel alone, but you are not alone. You are learning about yourself. You are growing. You are being shaped into the glorious creation of you, and in order to come out fully formed and solid on the other side, you must go through the fire of adolescence. You might feel awkward and ugly and wrong. You might feel like everyone else has it all figured out. You might feel shunned by the crowds who used to accept you. Similarly, you might look at those people and decide they are not the company you want to keep anymore. You might feel like nobody understands you, that you are too sensitive or too strange. You might feel crushingly alone.

This is not true.

Your peers all feel alone too. Your friends worry about how they look too. Even the girls who appear to have it all figured out—who seem popular and pretty and look like they have the world at their fingertips—feel just as worried and weird as you do sometimes. Nobody around you is more right in the world than you, nobody belongs more than you, nobody is better than you. And, more importantly, as a girl, you are part of a community, a source of experience, wisdom and brilliant wit that the women before you and around you have earned. We are all rooting for you.

You are not alone; you will never be alone.

Whatever you feel and whatever you fear, you are among friends.

I might throw the word "feminism" in here, and I want you to know what I mean when I use it. Basically, if the ideas in this book excite you and make you feel powerful and ready—even if you don't know yet what you are ready for—that's feminism in the pages. You should never be denied any opportunity simply because you are a girl. That's all it means. My personal brand of feminism also insists that: you should be allowed to feel excited and proud of your girlhood, should foster sisterhood instead of petty competition, should be always aware of the millions of possibilities waiting, hushed and giddy just beneath the surface.

I am a feminist, for one, because I couldn't be happy with myself without constantly acknowledging the strong women who, far before I came along, fought hard for the rights and recognition for themselves and for all the girls who would come after. That's you. That's me. I also just flat-out love being a girl and always have. Girls are complicated and fiery and mysterious. We have odds to overcome, every day, and every small victory makes us stronger, smarter and more interesting and funny. And that's why this book exists. The sooner that we start acknowledging those odds and calling them out for what they are—outdated ideas of girlhood! People threatened by challenging new ideas! Criminal companies harvesting dangerous insecurities so they can make a buck!—the sooner we can begin to destroy the odds, expand the dangerously small minds, and pave wider, brighter paths for ourselves and for the girls who will come after us.

So let's get started.

You don't need to be like everyone else. Why would you want to be? Most people are unhappy. Most people settle for less than they deserve, because they are afraid of being alone, and they are afraid of failure. But you—you know better than to settle for unhappiness.

Question everything. E-v-e-r-y-t-h-i-n-g. The things that are really true won't be lost. They are the ones that will survive the questioning.

You are influenced by the music you listen to, by the magazines you read and by the television you watch. The old saying goes that we are what we eat, but the definition is broader than that—we are what we *intake*, and that includes reality TV, Top 40 and sex tips in *Cosmo*. Choose your influences carefully, and do not simply accept the media that is fed to you. It is engineered to cripple you with insecurities. The world is wide, and the internet is even wider. Explore your options. Influence yourself. Choose to be empowered and educated.

Do more of what you love. That is, identify what you love to do. Once you do identify what you want to do, do it relentlessly. If you want to take photographs, carry a camera with you wherever you go, and never give yourself an opportunity to mourn missed chances for photos. Create a website for free and put your photos online, mail friends and family the link, graffiti it in bathrooms. If you love math, psychology, farming, science, fixing things—study it, go to the library and check out every book that looks exciting. Write letters to your mentors. Study the masters, study yourself, study your next-door neighbors. If you want to write, write in journals, write in book margins, write when you wake up in the middle of the night. Paste your writing down on paper and take yourself on a date to Kinko's to make a zine (or sneak some copies at your office job, if you have one—not that I have ever done that myself, a-hem). Give it to your friends, tuck it in strangers' backpacks, ask to sell copies on consignment at your favorite stores. Be relentless and unapologetic with your passion and with what you create, because nobody else will do it for you.

If nothing else, put out into the world what you yourself need from the world, and you will find that it's received gratefully by someone who needed it desperately. That's how this book came to exist.

Please, please, please, please, please masturbate. Learn about your body.

Sex in general is something that many people—possibly your parents, your preacher, or your school system—don't want to believe you need or are curious about, but I believe that you are, and I'm here to tell you that there is nothing wrong, dirty, or immoral about it. Seriously. Life is really short. Lock the door and look at yourself in a mirror; learn to identify every part, explore how it feels when each part is touched. Experiment. In the name of all the girls who never did—and there are plenty—learn to give yourself an orgasm—this is certainly a skill that will come in handy (pun definitely intended) for the absolute rest of your life, particularly the parts of your life when you can't sleep and there's nothing on TV. Honestly, lovers will come and go; it is essential that you are always able to love yourself foremost, in every conceivable way.

A note on feeling guilty about masturbation, whether your guilt comes from religion or not: when you touch certain parts of your body, it feels good. When you touch other parts of your body, it feels bad. Touching your eyeball, for example, hurts. Touching your clitoris generally feels nice. And that, my friends, is really all masturbation is. Not all people believe so, but it is not inherently bad or good. It is just a nerve and tissue response. I recommend you be a revolutionary, and give it a good old-fashioned try.

Don't freeze up about talking to your girlfriends about these things. I, for one, have always been fairly educated and open with my own body, but didn't discuss any bodily or sexual matters with my girlfriends until I was almost out of college. Once, when alone in a room with one of my best friends, she asked me point-blank if I ever masturbated and I shrugged and said no, and so she shrugged and did the same. We opened up to each other about these topics later that same year, but I still regret my reaction to her question. Why in the world did I say *no* when I could have replied, "Uh, you mean *today?*" and then had to count on my fingers? A lie only served to make us both feel more alone.

Listen: for some reason, there is a strong stigma against girls talking openly about their bodies, masturbation, orgasms, menstruation, and about enjoying sex. I am here to tell you that, for boys, sharing this kind of talk—even passing around pornography and then hanging around watching it together—is nearly a rite of passage in childhood. Can you imagine how much differently girls would approach sex—how much more open and unashamed the dialogue would be—if that were the standard for us from the beginning? Honest talk with your trusted friends

4

is always beneficial, no matter the subject matter; honest talk about otherwise hushed topics is even more essential. Destroy that (and every other) double standard. It's ludicrous.

So, sex. I really want to get this sex part right. Let's talk about it.

For girls, sex with another person is often made out to be a tender and sacred ceremony: you open your petals for your beloved; you sigh unanimously as your souls entwine and intermingle. And it isn't really like that. At least, with the right partner and the right intentions, it *can* be like that, if you both feel like synchronizing your gentle sighs. But the act of intercourse is not physically graceful. It's actually pretty ridiculous, and pathetic in the right light: two bodies clinging to each other, humping. But that's what is also so great about it—sex is embarrassing! In a society that wants us to be cool and aloof, sex is earnest and messy. You might make noises you never meant to make. You might start laughing or crying for no discernible reason. You might not know where to put your arms or what to say while you're doing it. You might also find that sex is painful or physically difficult for you. This is why it's important to do it with someone you trust: you and your sex partner will have to navigate all these things together.

And then, of course, there are some very serious sides to sex, such as STDs (sexually transmitted diseases) and the chance of pregnancy. These are literally not to be fucked with. And for years, upper management has struggled with telling you so. "How do we keep these kids from getting pregnant or getting AIDS in a way that's easy and convenient for *us?*" they ask. And the answer, somehow, has never been to plan and provide legit sex ed classes or information, free condoms and dams and birth control pills for all. The answer is to just lecture you to practice abstinence. "Hey," they say, as your bodies change and your hormones ramp and snort like bulls in a pen. "Hey. Don't have sex, k? You're not ready. Also, hot lunch today is meatloaf surprise."

I know the infinite, untouchable feeling that comes with being young. I remember acknowledging it directly, when I was 16, speeding on desolate country roads in my silver '93 Lumina. The radio was loud, the moon was swollen and lit above me, I was traveling back home from a boyfriend's, and everything was awesome. I felt young and limitless and untouchable. It wasn't until six years later, when a driver fell asleep at the wheel and smashed headlong into me on a similarly desolate interstate, that I realized how it all works. See, I couldn't have seen the wreck coming. I was driving to get from one place to another. And I wasn't the one who fell asleep while driving. I wasn't the one who drifted across three lanes of highway. But I was the one *who had worn my seat belt.* And I escaped a deadly wreck with nothing more than lots of cuts and bruises, and broken glass in my hair.

This is a metaphor I'm making here.

If you are having sex, you are using condoms. It is *so easy* to use condoms. Carry a couple with you, in a backpack or a purse—doing so does not make you presumptuous or slutty, it makes you prepared, forward-thinking and responsible. Better yet, use a highly effective method of birth control (and *no,* pulling out at the last second does not count) along with condoms at all times.

Planned Parenthood has been an essential tool for me in learning about my sexual health, and it is one I warmly believe in and recommend. It is the only resource I know of that provides quality healthcare and unbiased education to women regardless of income, age or social status. If you are having sex, or thinking about having sex, I advise you to go online and find the PP clinic closest to you. They can give you free condoms, educate you on the ins and outs (so to speak) of having sex, and aid you in obtaining birth control. They are the legit sex ed course that most schools stubbornly refuse to provide. They also have health care professionals available to answer your questions in a myriad of ways (including texts from your phone)—see the Resources section at the end of the book.

There is no "safe" level when it comes to inflicting harm on yourself. That goes for abusing yourself mentally (calling yourself stupid, obsessing over mistakes), torturing yourself emotionally (making decisions you know are unhealthy, sacrificing your worth for a relationship), and for hurting yourself physically. Self-injury in young girls is still a taboo topic in most circles, maybe by nature—it's a secret habit, fueled by shame, kept bandaged underneath long sleeves and pant legs. Yet it is a habit that feeds upon itself, perpetuated by the silence and fear it creates. There are many professional resources available to help you if you are a self-injurer, and I am not one of those resources (please see the appropriate section at the back of the book). Please know that you are not alone. In fact, you are hardly alone at all.

It makes me so angry to know the long-standing statistics of self-injury: overwhelmingly, girls do it more than boys, and overwhelmingly, girls are beginning to hurt themselves at younger ages. And those things are true for a reason: there is just simply too much pressure.

You are not responsible for anyone else's feelings but your own. Your own feelings are all real and true and valid and should never be stifled for anyone else's convenience. You are an equal. You deserve happiness—not just happiness that hobbles alongside you, but brilliant, overwhelming happiness that shines within your skin. You are powerful and brave enough to ask for it, to demand it, and one brief moment of believing that—right now—is all it takes to receive it.

Be nice to anyone who brings you your food, carries your bags or drives you around. Always tip 20% (rule of thumb: move the decimal point on your bill one space to the left, then double that for the tip). Always write thank-you cards. Always leave five minutes early in order to be on time. Always call home when you will be out late. Always repeat someone's name when you are introduced to them.

No one will ever make you happy except for you. No boy, no girl, no parents, no hobby or sunny day or expensive trinket is going to be able to fill a void inside you until you fill that void up yourself. Listen to yourself first and foremost. Love yourself first and foremost.

If someone bores you, he or she is not worth your time. The same goes for someone hurting you, mocking you, dismissing your feelings, ignoring you, or manipulating you.

If you are dating someone, make it a point to continue to plan regular solo dates with your friends. When your relationship ends, you don't want to pop your head up for air only to realize that you have let all your dear friendships drift. Give your time to the people you care about.

On the other side of that coin, if you are friends with someone who is continually ditching you for her new fling, speak up. It's no big deal; just tell her that you miss her and that you'd like to schedule some quality time. It's very easy—no matter how old you are—to live in a bubble when you're in a relationship. But by continuing to pursue your own outside interests, maintain your own friendships, and work toward your own goals, you become a stronger and more interesting person. Too many people give up on being all that interesting.

Listen, high school ladies who have a boyfriend: don't marry your boyfriend. I know that if you're even considering it right now, this advice is lost on you because you've heard the statistics and are still convinced that you and your man can make it; you're shaking your head even as you're reading this because you two are the one exception to the rule. But I don't give you this warning because of statistics; I give you this warning because you have a long and wondrous life ahead of you, and it will be filled with places and people you can't possibly imagine yet. Plus, that man you're in love with now isn't a man—he's a boy. He is perhaps wonderful, perhaps particularly so, I know you love him, and I believe that love is real and beautiful, but you are too precious and the road is too wide and wondrous to bind yourself in any way while there is still so much left to come. When you feel it is time to move on, tell him the truth, thank him for being your first love (something you will always have between you), and immediately make a huge, sprawling list of things you want to do, places you want to live, things you want to learn in your life. This person will change, and so will you (and thank goodness for growth), and you will develop new interests and you will move to different locations and you will become different people.

Read this again in five years and initial if I was right: _____. Then search me out and let me know, because I *love* being right.

Listen, high school ladies who don't have a boyfriend: you are not the only one who doesn't have a boyfriend. I know it feels like you are sometimes, and maybe it's something that makes you feel like you're missing out. Your journey, though, is still your own, and you will never be as young, alive, or free as you are right now.

Listen, high school ladies who have a girlfriend: I hope you will be free to marry your girlfriend someday, no matter where you live. That said, see above. If you do choose to marry later in life, and it is this person that you wed, then I will stand up at your wedding and throw flowers and cry into my champagne during your first dance. Seat me at the fun table, please. No boring aunts or creepy uncles.

Broken hearts are the worst. A broken heart is real; it is valid and tangible; it hurts and hurts and never stops hurting until one day, when you realize it hurts less. The only way over it is through. I wish this weren't the case and I'm sorry.

No matter how much you want to be friends with your ex-beloved right after a break-up, do not try. It is too hard and unfair to be worth it. You will *want* to try. For every break-up as long as you live, there will be a million songs on the radio or funny stories or little heartbreaking things that will make you think, "That person is the only one who would appreciate this with me." It isn't true. There are always more people than you think—more wonderful, silly, funny and heartbreaking people. Keep your distance from one another after a break-up, for longer than you think could possibly be necessary. I'm talking no e-mails, no texts, no nothing. It will go against your instincts at first, and it will probably feel horrible and cruel and lonely, but it will also help. You have to grieve in your own way so that you can recover in your own way.

Remember: just because a break-up is painful doesn't mean that it isn't also right.

Don't be too wary of talking to adults about issues or problems that feel particularly sensitive, particularly personal and your own. You will likely be surprised to discover the similar threads and themes that run through all our lives. Cling to the wise people you meet. Don't take them for granted.

Explore. Read more books. Turn off the computer. Keep a journal. Listen to people when they talk to you. Take notes.

Procrastination is nothing more than a voice inside you telling you that you are not good enough to accomplish a goal. Overcoming it is not always easy, but it is extremely possible. Try to be practical, and set a timer for, say, twenty minutes of work at a time, for starters. Then decide to believe—even for one second of those twenty minutes, all it takes to get started—that you deserve to give yourself the hard work and time to do your best. Then you let the timer tick. Reward yourself each time you reach a goal, however small.

The biggest problem with saying "like" before and between every word isn't just that it's, like, annoying and abrasive. The real problem is that it dilutes the importance of your words. Girls are much more likely than boys to invalidate their own thoughts—pay attention to it the next time you're in class and hear someone say, "Um, like, Romeo kinda like—he thought Juliet was, like, dead? So he, like, killed himself? Too?" when she really means, "Yo. Romeo thought Juliet was dead, so he committed suicide. Next question." Watch your *like*s, your *kinda*s and *sorta*s, your *um*s, *uh*s and *I dunno*s. They precede the substance of what you say. If you are making a statement, don't end it with a question mark. Do not minimize your intelligence, your work, nor your instincts. They are all valid, essential and important. You know what you're trying to say even when you don't have the words. Don't give anyone a reason to not take you seriously. You are brilliant and capable, and your thoughts are worth anyone's time.

Some people—namely dudes, for some reason—find it okay to yell supposedly flattering things at other people—namely, ladies—as they pass these people on the street. My only educated guess is that people do these things because they can. That said, do not trust people who do things just because they can.

On the topic of alcohol, let me give the light advice before the heavy advice: once you drink enough to give yourself a hangover the next morning, you can never go back. Hangovers are miserable. Practice tolerance from the beginning. Your liver, your head, your stomach, and your friends will thank you.

Try to be completely informed of the effects of anything you put into your system. That goes for food, that goes for medicine, and that goes for anything recreational. As for drugs and alcohol, realize exactly what they are—mind-alterers—and don't let them become anything more than that, a crutch or a portal to any wonderful brilliant new land. When they wear off, you will return to the same world and be the same person you were before (unless we're talking acid trips or meth binges, in which case you may not return at all, and in which case I am no longer an acceptable advisor). Retain the ability to look at yourself and your choices objectively, out of context of a sloshed Saturday night out, and don't dive into these vices headlong. If you are feeling like you might be losing control of yourself to drinking or drugs, or if you are seeking help who a friend who is, please see the Resources section toward the end of the book.

Be aware of your surroundings. Whether you are in class, driving downtown, or walking home at night, this must be the case. When walking to your car at night, keep your keys in your hand. Always walk confidently, with your chin up. Look around you as you walk, and do not hesitate to act on your instincts. If a situation feels wrong or scary, it is because your brain and body are picking up clues that may signal danger.

You cannot stop life from being unpredictable and sometimes scary. But you can be the one who wears the seat belt. The one who carries the condoms. The one who speaks up when she feels threatened or compromised. The one who keeps her head up and her eyes and ears open.

Always be aware when someone is trying to sell you something. People are going to tell you, directly and indirectly, that you're not thin enough, not smooth enough, not tan enough, not dressed right; they throw images of supposed perfection at you because if they can keep you feeling small, not quite good enough, then chances are higher that they'll make money off you. It is right and smart to be dubious of this practice; it is widely accepted and chronically widespread. In other words, fuck that.

Your period isn't gross or dirty or bad and anyone who tries to make you feel otherwise is trying to sell you something. Yes, it's often painful and messy, but we are mammals just a few evolutionary steps past living in a nest of our own shit. Your period is a rare reminder that your body is a body, not something you can control. Make it a point to be good to yourself; take it easy on your body. Don't believe anyone who tries to make you feel as if your period is something dirty and bad that should be ignored or done away with as quickly as possible (lots of people make money from the sales of scented, tiny tampons; just sayin')—be dubious of anything and anyone who recommends their product as an alternative to something your body *does*. Your body grows hair and gets sweaty and sticky and your uterus sheds its lining once every month or so. It is your right to deal with those facts in whatever way you want.

Get into the habit of never allowing yourself to compare yourself negatively—your grades, your money, your body, your jokes, your accomplishments or your clothes—to anyone else. This is a hard habit to stop. Keep a rubber band on your wrist and snap it every time you think a negative thought about yourself and your mind will eventually begin respond in classic Pavlovian form.

Other people's opinions of you are none of your business. You are you, not anyone else, and you are on your own particular journey. Strive to make that journey as exciting, positive, fun and adventurous as you desire and deserve. On that same note, realize that the girl next to you is trying to figure things out as well, and it's just as confusing and difficult and thrilling for her as it is for you. Sometimes people make choices that seem awful. Try not to be too harsh with your judgments.

Remember this every time you worry about what people are thinking when they hear you, see you, or think of you. The only person who can "make" you feel anything—including unworthy and out-of-place—is you. As for anybody else's opinions, you simply choose how to respond to them. Decide that you operate on a level that is not bothered by anyone else's opinion, and suddenly, a dark veil lifts. You begin to live for your own happiness.

Dress with confidence. Every day, dress in whatever makes you feel however you want to feel. The secret to fashion doesn't lie in the cut of your skirt or in what "season" your skin tone is or in horizontal or vertical stripes. The only secret to fashion is this: if you wear it with confidence, if you *wear* it and believe in it, then you can pull it off.

Widen your vision of what beauty is. Realize and keep close the fact that a beauty standard has been created by the very people who sell it, and that it is no accident that the accepted "beauty standard" can easily be described as "perfect." Flaws are not tolerated if you want to be perfect. But the models that we see most often—even the tallest and thinnest and most doe-eyed—are still pinned and sprayed and pulled into place. Then they are manipulated digitally until, literally, everything that might be perceived as a "flaw" is erased. This is a way to sell product. It has nothing to do with real life. It has nothing to do with you. We are made of so-called "flaws." They are the thread that stitches our parts together and keeps us from being generic cut-out paper dolls. You are beautiful. You are enough, now and always. You have always been enough.

Learn to accept a genuine compliment with grace instead of denial. Say simply "thank you," and smile.

Give random compliments to strangers—or not-so-random compliments to not-so-strangers. If you love someone's scarf or dress or the compelling speech she gave in class, say so. This is especially gratifying with other girls, since we are so socialized to compete with each other, to be jealous and petty with one another. When you level this playing field and take yourself out of the game, you identify yourself as a friend—one confident enough to lift up and encourage others, instead of cutting them down. Create and foster sisterhood among the girls you know, not petty competition. The more we cut each other down, the lower we all sink into jealousy and insecurity. There is no need for us to push each other out of the way. There is more than enough attention, excitement and love for each of us.

Stop using "fat" as an insult. It isn't one. It's a descriptor, like saying you're a brunette, or that you're wearing a bright red shirt. Don't use it as an insult in describing each other, and don't use it as an insult when describing yourself.

When you get a zit—and if you don't get pimples, never make fun of anyone who does, because you *will* get a dose of karmic zit revenge—put toothpaste on it before bed. Not the gel kind. Something with baking soda. Leave it on overnight and, hey, try to remember to wash it off in the morning.

Your body needs water, fruits, vegetables, and lots of protein. Them's the facts. We are animals, our bodies are mammal bodies, and if it comes from the Earth, it's compatible with our earthly selves. If you are going to spend extra money or extra time on something, consider letting it be the food that you put into your body, the only one you will ever have. Strive to eat locally, from farms and butchers in the area. Learn what produce is in season—it's been flown across the world otherwise, and plane tickets ain't cheap, even for an orange.

Don't stop playing. Crawl around on the floor. Hang upside-down off your couch and imagine the ceiling is the floor. Stretch. Swing. Yell. Jump. Before too long, you will forget how it felt to run and scream and tumble as a kid would, and that's a sad skill to lose.

If God exists, the only things I am sure of are that 1) God loves us with every flaw included (Grace Bauer calls them our "small human details"), 2) we can talk to this Almighty any way we want or try, and also that 3) She is not an old white man.

It's a miracle that you are here and that the person next to you is here. That your father's and mother's bodily fluids combined in such a way to shape your face, your ribcage, the arches of your feet—that is the place where textbook science and impossible miracles meet. Your existence is even more beautiful and improbable each day, as you continue to not get hit by cars, not trip and bust your skull, not puncture your eardrum with a Q-tip after a morning shower. Realize and appreciate that fact.

Make a conscious effort, every day, to better yourself. Don't ignore the lessons that life teaches you; tuck them in your pocket and carry them with you, spread them like flower seeds to eventually take root and bloom for others. Be brave. Teach yourself. Do things you can't do. You make your own life and write your own story; the sooner you realize that fact, the more joyful and powerful your choices will be. And always choose love. Whatever the other choice is, it is utterly inferior when sized up next to love. (If you are not sure which is love, here is a guide: love is the most selfless choice.)

You are loved. You are desperately wanted. You are brilliant and beautiful and you deserve everything for which you are brave enough to ask. You don't have it figured out; you won't ever have it figured out, but if you equip yourself with the tools to tear through your life bravely, unabashedly and with grace, you'll have it figured out as anyone, and you will come out better, stronger and sweeter because of it.

A general rule of thumb for living: if the only thing holding you back is that you feel like you can't do it, do it.

Oh, and if you ever ride the MTD in Champaign-Urbana, Illinois—to open the back door, you just press on the door handle. For some reason there are signs and directions that instruct you on how to do everything but that. Allow me to spare you the embarrassment I had to live through. Woof.

Abuse

Anti-Hate Line
A service, partnered with the Human Relations Commission, for listening, reporting, and follow-up of incidences of discrimination and hate crimes.
800-649-0404

ChildHelp USA
800-422-4453

National Teen Dating Abuse Helpline
1-866-331-9474
Live chat at http://www.loveisrespect.org/

National Domestic Violence Hotline
Crisis intervention, information and referrals.
866-331-9474
(English and Spanish)

Self-Injury Hotline
800-DONT CUT (1-800-366-8288)

SAFE (Self Abuse Finally Ends) Alternatives Program
www.selfinjury.com

Drugs/Alcohol

Al-Anon/Alateen Hotline
Hope & help for young relatives & friends of a problem drinker.
800-344-2666

Substance Abuse Treatment Locator
http://findtreatment.samhsa.gov/
800-662-4357

Eating Disorders

National Association of Anorexia Nervosa and Associated Disorders
Hotline, Counseling and Referrals
847-831-3438

Gay, Lesbian, Bisexual, and Transgender (GLBT) Youth Support Line
800-850-8078

CDC National AIDS/Sexually Transmitted Disease Hotline
Information and referral. (24 Hours)

800-342-2437 (English)
800-227-8922 (English/Spanish)
800-344-7432 (Spanish)
800-243-7889 (TTY)

Planned Parenthood
Speak to a health educator.
877.4ME.2ASK.
Monday - Friday
9 a.m. - 6 p.m. (PST)

Live chat
www.plannedparenthoodchat.org

Text questions to 53634

TalkZone (Peer Counselors)
800-475-TALK (1-800-475-2855)

National Adolescent Suicide Hotline
800-621-4000

Ani Difranco, Kimya Dawson, Brother Ali, Liz Phair (*whitechocolatespaceegg* and earlier), Patti Smith, The Gossip, Yeah Yeah Yeahs, Peaches, Bikini Kill, Loretta Lynn, Of Montreal, Fiona Apple, Nellie McKay, Curb Service, Mos Def.

RECOMMENDED FICTION.

listed in general order of reading difficulty

- Harriet's Daughter, Marlene Philip
- Ella Enchanted, Gail Carson Levine
- Catherine, Called Birdy, Karen Cushman
- The Disreputable History of Frankie Landau-Banks, Emily Lockhart
- Hard Love, Ellen Wittlinger
- Are You There, God? It's Me, Margaret, Judy Blume
- Jellicoe Road, Melina Marchetta
- The House on Mango Street, Sandra Cisneros
- Girl Goddess #9, Francesca Lia Block
- Coraline, Neil Gaiman
- Oranges Are Not the Only Fruit, Jeanette Winterson
- Flaming Iguanas: An All-Girl Road Novel Thing, Erika Lopez
- The Awakening, Kate Chopin
- Their Eyes Were Watching God, Zora Neale Hurston
- Mrs. Dalloway, Virginia Woolf
- The Bluest Eye, Toni Morrison
- The Handmaid's Tale, Margaret Atwood

Health / Sexuality

* Changing Bodies, Changing Lives: A Book for Teens on Sex and Relationships, Ruth Bell
* Our Bodies, Ourselves: A New Edition for a New Era, The Boston Women's Health Book Collective
* S.E.X.: The All-You-Need-To-Know Progressive Sexuality Guide to Get You Through High School and College, Heather Corinna
* Deal with It!: A Whole New Approach to Your Body, Brain, and Life as a gURL, Esther Drill, Heather McDonald, Rebecca Odes
* The Period Book, Updated Edition: Everything You Don't Want to Ask (But Need to Know), Karen Gravelle
* GLBTQ: The Survival Guide for Queer and Questioning Teens, Kelly Huegel
* Cunt: A Declaration of Independence, Inga Muscio

Zines

* Zine Scene: The Do It Yourself Guide to Zines, Francesca Lia Block, Hillary Carlip
* Make a Zine! When Words and Graphics Collide, Bill Brent, Joe Biel
* Invincible Summer & Invincible Summer II, Nicole Georges (anthologies of my favorite zine)
* A Girl's Guide to Taking over the World: Writings from the Girl Zine Revolution, edited by Karen Green and Tristan Taormino
* Whatcha Mean, What's a Zine?, Esther Watson
* Stolen Sharpie Revolution 2: A DIY Resource for Zines and Zine Culture, Alex Wrekk, Nicole Introvert

- Listen Up: Voices from the Next Feminist Generation, edited by Barbara Findlen
- Spilling Open: The Art of Becoming Yourself, Sabrina Ward Harrison
- Colonize This!: Young Women of Color on Today's Feminism, edited by Daisy Hernandez and Bushra Rehman
- The Bust Guide to the New Girl Order, edited by Marcelle Karp and Debbie Stoller
- Pretty in Punk: Girl's Gender Resistance in a Boy's Subculture, Lauraine Leblanc
- Reviving Ophelia: Saving the Selves of Adolescent Girls, Mary Pipher
- Rock 'n' Roll Camp for Girls: How to Start a Band, Write Songs, Record an Album, and Rock Out!, Rock 'n' Roll Camp for Girls

Memoir/Essays

- Slouching Toward Bethlehem, Joan Didion
- The Vagina Monologues, Eve Ensler
- Traveling Mercies, Anne Lamott
- Persepolis, Marjane Satrapi

Magazines

- *Bust*
- *Bitch*
- *Ms.*
- *Zoetrope: All-Story*
- *ReadyMade*

Thank you to everyone who read this book in its first incarnation, as a sewn paper zine with a hot pink cover. Thank you to everyone who wrote to me and said thank you; thank you to everyone who wrote to me and said she was excited for the book, or who asked about the book, or who donated money toward the publication of the book. This is for you. You made it happen. It would not exist without you, because it is you.

Thank you to my mother. Thank you to my grandmas, Marilyn Lynch and Janet Markel. Thank you to my aunts Julie and Jayne. Thank you, L'Aux, my gang of strange girls. Thank you, Larry E. Gates II, my dear and radical heart. Thank you Syddo, proof that people are innately good. Thank you, Kelly and Kaitlin and Angelina. Thank you, Laura Jane Faulds, thank you Jessalyn Wakefield. Thank you, Rachel Corrie. Thank you, Ani Difranco (*coolest f-word ever deserves a fuckin' shout!*), thank you, Anne Lamott. Thank you, Kimya Dawson. Thank you, Ariel Gore. Thank you, school teachers. Thank you, Mark Willhardt. Thank you, Pauline Kayes. Thank you, *Bitch* magazine. Thank you, Kickstarter.com.

Thank you to the zine community. Thank you to all the other girls who were online coding their own websites in the mid-90s.

Thank you so much, Nicole Johnston (killmargot.com), who designed the gorgeous artwork for the book.

Thank you.

YOUR NOTES.

(What do you love most about you? About your friends?
What are you most knowledgeable about?

What makes you uniquely beautiful?
Who is a person you admire? Why do you admire him/her?

Write your list of goals, things you want to learn, places
you will explore, books to read, people to meet.)

Lindsey Markel is a writer and actress in Champaign, Illinois. This is her first book.

youareamongfriends.com

NOLITE TE BASTARDES CARBORUNDORUM.

Made in the USA
San Bernardino, CA
06 July 2016